Original title:
Silent Sands

Copyright © 2024 Swan Charm
All rights reserved.

Author: Kätriin Kaldaru
ISBN HARDBACK: 978-9908-1-2587-9
ISBN PAPERBACK: 978-9908-1-2588-6
ISBN EBOOK: 978-9908-1-2589-3

The Lullaby of the Dusty Trail

The soft wind sings a tune,
Beneath the silver moon.
Footprints blend with the soil,
As night embraces the toil.

Stars whisper secrets low,
In the soft evening glow.
The trail hums with old tales,
Of laughter that still prevails.

Crickets join the serenade,
In shadows softly laid.
Gentle sighs of the trees,
Match the rhythm of the breeze.

Pathways twist, dreams unfold,
In the whispers of the bold.
Life's echoes softly play,
On the lullaby of the day.

So let the night unwind,
With treasures intertwined.
Nature's song, sweet and clear,
Guides the heart ever near.

Fragrant Memories in the Heat Haze

Golden fields stretch afar,
Underneath the sun's scar.
Warmth wraps the world in glow,
As scents of life freely flow.

Lavender dances in breeze,
Whispers carried with ease.
Moments caught in the air,
Like dreams we all can share.

The heat shimmers with grace,
Memory's gentle embrace.
Time dances on this land,
As honey drips from the hand.

Footsteps trace where we roam,
In this fragrant sweet home.
Fleeting scents pull us tight,
Through the corridors of light.

Each flower tells a tale,
In the warmth we set sail.
Through the haze, joy sparks bright,
Fragrant memories take flight.

The Palette of Nature's Quiet

Soft pastels paint the dawn,
As silent hues are drawn.
Brushstrokes of emerald leaves,
Whisper secrets nature weaves.

Golden yellows softly blend,
As day begins to send.
A canvas vast and wide,
With hues that thrive and abide.

Cerulean skies unfold,
Stories yet to be told.
Crimson sunsets ignite,
Trailing dreams through the night.

Each color holds a sigh,
In the whispers of the sky.
Nature's palette reigns clear,
Inviting all hearts near.

Through tranquil strokes of grace,
Time finds its rightful place.
In the quiet, we see,
The beauty of simply be.

Echoing Dreams Beneath Timeless Skies

Stars flicker with delight,
In the cloak of the night.
Dreams drift on whispered air,
Floating softly, beyond care.

Moonlight casts its silver net,
On paths where hearts have met.
Every shadow tells a tale,
In the night's gentle veil.

Whispers travel through the void,
Bringing memories enjoyed.
Time lingers, softly sways,
In the echoes of our days.

Beneath the arching blue,
Faded dreams come into view.
With every shining spark,
We embrace the endless dark.

In the tapestry of night,
Hope ignites with pure light.
Timeless dreams, forever soar,
Beneath the sky's open door.

Whispers of the Desert Twilight

The sun dips low, the shadows grow,
A gentle breeze begins to flow.
Stars awaken in the deepening hue,
As night unravels its cloak anew.

The sands reflect the evening's glow,
Footsteps soft where whispers go.
Secrets shared beneath the sky,
In twilight's breath, dreams flutter by.

Cacti reach for the dusky light,
Guardians of the velvet night.
The moon takes stage in silver dress,
Soft secrets in the wilderness.

Echoes Beneath the Dune

Soft echoes dance on shifting sand,
Footprints lost, fate unplanned.
Stories buried deep within,
Waiting for the night to begin.

Through the dunes, the murmurs slide,
Ancient tales that time can't hide.
Each rustle holds a point in time,
Nature's rhythm, a silent rhyme.

The stars above spark stories bright,
Guiding wanderers through the night.
Voices rise with the desert wind,
In haunting echoes, past rescinds.

Secrets in the Grit

Underneath the barren sky,
Lies the grit where secrets lie.
Each grain a memory held tight,
Stories whispered in the night.

What lies buried will resurface,
In the dawn, the sun's good service.
The winds may scatter tales anew,
Yet in the core, the past rings true.

Hidden treasures in the dust,
Time reveals what's understood.
The grit remembers every ghost,
In silent vigil, it will boast.

Murmurs of the Grain

Fields of gold, the waves do play,
Each stalk sways in soft ballet.
The whispers of the harvest call,
In nature's song, we hear it all.

Voices carried on the breeze,
Rustling softly through the trees.
A tale of growth, of toil and time,
Nature's rhythm, a gentle chime.

As dusk descends, it starts to fade,
The silken whispers softly made.
In every grain a story spun,
The heart of earth, a song begun.

The Loneliness of Endless Horizons

Where the sky meets the sea,
A whisper in the breeze,
Lonely sails drift afar,
Chasing dreams with ease.

Clouds gather, heavy and gray,
Marking time in silence,
Each wave a heart's soft sigh,
Yearning for a balance.

In the distance, shadows play,
Fleeting moments in light,
Distant cries of unseen birds,
Lost in endless flight.

The sun dips low on the edge,
Painting skies orange and red,
Where the earth kisses the ocean,
And dreams are softly fed.

In the quiet of twilight's song,
Loneliness softly stirs,
For every horizon reached,
Another one occurs.

Ceremonials of the Dusty Earth

Under the sun's harsh gaze,
The earth holds ancient tales,
Whispers of the winds that passed,
And time that never fails.

Beneath a sky of faded gray,
Dust dances in the light,
Each grain a memory etched,
In shadows of the night.

Nature's drum beats steady on,
In rhythms worn and old,
Ceremonies of life unfold,
In stories yet untold.

Roots dig deep, seek their truth,
Branches stretch toward the vast,
In earthy prayers and offerings,
We connect with the past.

The cycle spins, day to day,
With each sunset and dawn,
The dusty earth remembers still,
What once was and is gone.

Breath of the Awakening Desert

In the hush of dawn's first light,
The desert stirs awake,
Golden sands and whispering winds,
A world begins to shake.

Cacti stretch, their arms up high,
Embracing morning's grace,
While shadows slowly melt away,
In the sun's warm embrace.

Life flickers, fragile yet bold,
In a realm where dreams abound,
Each pulse of wind a silent song,
In the stillness, profound.

Mirages dance on the horizon,
With secrets yet untold,
As the desert breathes anew,
In colors bright and bold.

With every grain of shifting sand,
Life finds a way to thrive,
In the heart of the awakening,
Where the spirit comes alive.

The Quiet Lament of the Landscape

Mountains stand like ancient guards,
Witnesses to the time,
In valleys deep, the echoes speak,
Of a past that feels like rhyme.

Rivers carve through hardened stone,
Whispering to the trees,
The quiet lament of nature's heart,
Carried on the breeze.

Fields of gold sway gently slow,
In the twilight's fading hue,
Memories of all who tread upon,
Each path both old and new.

The sky weeps, in colors soft,
As the sun bids farewell,
To the landscapes rich with stories,
In their silence, they dwell.

So listen close to nature's voice,
In the heart of the earth,
For every sigh and every sound,
Carries a tale of worth.

The Elegy of an Unseen Oasis

In the heart of the barren sand,
Whispers of water softly yearn,
Beneath the hot sun's heavy hand,
A secret world in shadows churn.

Winds of time have buried dreams,
Fading echoes of laughter lost,
Where silence reigns and stillness beams,
A place of solace, at what cost?

The palm trees bend with weary grace,
Longing for a gentle breeze,
In this forgotten, sacred space,
A dance of leaves on tempered seas.

Mirage of hope, it calls to me,
Yet I can never reach its core,
The cruel joke of fate, you see,
An oasis I can't explore.

Eternal thirst in endless night,
As stars above begin to weep,
A vision lost, out of my sight,
I wander on, forever deep.

Flickers of Hope in the Dust Storm

Amidst the chaos of swirling tides,
In the clutches of despair,
Flickers of hope like fireflies,
Illuminate the heavy air.

Each gust of wind, a tale unwinds,
Of battles fought and dreams anew,
Through the veil of dust, love finds,
A path to pierce the muted blue.

In shadows cast by fleeting storms,
Resilience breathes, a quiet sound,
With every heartbeat, courage warms,
From ashes, greater strength is found.

The horizon teases with its glow,
A promise held in fragile hands,
With every step, we learn to grow,
Together through these shifting sands.

So let the tempest rage and swirl,
For within the heart, a spark will glow,
In the eye of the storm, we can twirl,
As flickers of hope in dust storms flow.

Time's Gentle Caress on Lonely Terrain

On this stretch of silent earth,
Where shadows dance and dreams converge,
Time holds secrets of rebirth,
In every whisper, love's surge.

Mountains rise with ancient grace,
Stories etched in stone and soil,
Softly time begins to trace,
The lines of joy, of pain, of toil.

Each moment slips like grains of sand,
Yet in their fall, new worlds awake,
Time cradles dreams within its hand,
A gentle touch, a tender ache.

Beneath the stars, the echoes sing,
Of journeys bold and losses dear,
In solitude, new hope takes wing,
With every tick, it draws us near.

As the sun dips low in the sky,
Time paints the horizon red and gold,
In this lonely terrain, we sigh,
For moments lost and stories told.

Lament of a Withered Blossom

In the garden's heart, a bloom once bright,
Now crumbles under weight of years,
A withered blossom, lost to night,
Its petals fall like uncried tears.

Time has stolen vibrant hues,
Leaving traces of what had been,
Whispers of scent, a fading muse,
In the echoes of a landscape green.

Once, it danced with the morning light,
Now shadows drape its weary soul,
In the silence of vanished night,
The ache of absence takes its toll.

Yet hope resides in each dry stem,
As roots hold firm beneath the ground,
A promise that it may bloom again,
In the gentle touch of spring unbound.

For every withered petal falls,
A memory held in the earth's embrace,
Lament sings through the garden walls,
As life prepares for its sweet grace.

Where the Horizon Meets Solitude

The sun dips low, the sky aglow,
Whispers of winds, where soft dreams flow.
A barren path, a shadowed trace,
In quiet hearts, we find our place.

Mountains loom, silent and vast,
Moments linger, shadows cast.
Each footfall echoes, a gentle sigh,
Beneath the realm of the endless sky.

The world retreats, a whispering hush,
Nature's breath in the fading brush.
Stars emerge, a twinkling glance,
In solitude's embrace, we dance.

The horizon bends, a soft embrace,
In this stillness, we find our grace.
A canvas painted with vibrant hues,
Where solitude sings in softest blues.

A Canvas of Dust and Echoes

Beneath the sun, the earth lies bare,
Footprints left in the warming air.
Echoes linger, stories told,
Of ancient quests and hearts of gold.

Dust swirls gently, a ghostly veil,
Each grain a secret, a whispered tale.
In shadows long, the past remains,
A dance of history in endless chains.

The wind carries songs of the lost,
Through quiet valleys, a gentle frost.
Moments captured, forever cling,
In layers of dust, the echoes sing.

Time unfolds in the evening light,
With every step, the day turns night.
A canvas drawn with earth and sighs,
Where every heartbeat softly lies.

Starlit Quietude

The night drapes softly, a velvet cloak,
In silence deep, the stars evoke.
Each twinkle dances, a distant spark,
Guiding dreams through the quiet dark.

Moonlit whispers, a gentle breeze,
Swaying branches, rustling leaves.
Time takes pause under cosmic light,
In starlit quietude, hearts take flight.

A journey begins in the hush of night,
Where shadows blend and spirits ignite.
Together we wander, in silence that flows,
Through secret worlds as the starlight glows.

Wrapped in peace, the universe sighs,
Each twinkle a promise of endless skies.
In quietude deep, we find our way,
Guided by starlight, where dreams will stay.

The Language of Forgotten Lands

In relics worn, the stories blend,
Whispers of old where shadows mend.
Ancient stones in the fading light,
Hold secrets tight in the quiet night.

Voices echo from times long past,
Lost in the breezes that everlast.
Each rustle tells of journeys made,
Across the fields where spirits played.

In forgotten lands, the heartbeats thrum,
Over hills where the wildflowers hum.
Nature speaks in a timeless tongue,
In every breeze, a song is sung.

We listen close to the tales of yore,
In every sigh, a world to explore.
The language calls from the depths of time,
An ode of dreams, a silent rhyme.

The Stillness of Time's Embrace

In the quiet hour, shadows play,
Whispers of light begin to sway.
Moments linger, softly caught,
Fleeting memories, time forgot.

The clock ticks slow, a gentle sigh,
Eternity waits, as days drift by.
Each heartbeat echoes, sweetly near,
In the stillness, all becomes clear.

Waves of silence, touch the soul,
Every breath, a story whole.
Here in the pause, we find our way,
In time's embrace, we long to stay.

With every glance, the world unfolds,
Hidden wonders begin to mold.
In twilight's glow, the heart finds grace,
In the depth of time's embrace.

So let us dwell in this serene place,
Where shadows dance and dreams interlace.
For in each moment, still and bright,
We capture time in the fading light.

Echoes of the Desert Night

Beneath the stars, the cool winds blow,
Whispers of sand, a soft, low glow.
Cacti stand tall, a solemn sight,
Guardians of dreams in the desert night.

The moon hangs low, a silver thread,
Guiding the lost where few have tread.
Crickets sing their symphony sweet,
Nature's lullaby, a rhythmic beat.

Shadows dance on the dunes' embrace,
Time suspends in this endless space.
Every grain tells a tale untold,
Of ancient paths, brave and bold.

The fire's crackle, warmth so near,
Stories shared, laughter and cheer.
In the stillness, the heart takes flight,
Lost in the magic of the desert night.

As dawn approaches, the stars will fade,
But memories linger of dreams we've made.
Forever held in the quiet's might,
Echoes resound in the desert night.

Tranquil Shores of Forgotten Dreams

Upon the sands, soft waves caress,
Tales of yore, the tides confess.
Shells whisper secrets of days gone by,
Echoes of laughter under the sky.

The sun dips low, a fiery crown,
Painting the waves with hues of brown.
Footprints linger, washed away,
Memories drift, as night greets day.

Seagulls cry in the evening's breath,
Dancing lightly, defying death.
Here on the shore, time unravels,
In the stillness, the spirit travels.

The breeze carries dreams yet unspun,
In this haven, we become as one.
With every wave, our worries cease,
Finding solace, a gentle peace.

As stars emerge, the sky ignites,
A canvas of wonder on tranquil nights.
In these moments, our hearts will gleam,
On the shores of forgotten dreams.

Beneath the Veil of Twilight

As day surrenders to the night,
Shadows blossom, soft and bright.
The sun's last kiss, a faint goodbye,
Beneath the veil, the dreams will fly.

Colors blend in a whispered song,
A transition sweet, where we belong.
Stars awaken, begin to twinkle,
In the dusk, our hearts will crinkle.

The air grows cool, the world slows down,
In silence wrapped, we shed the crown.
Lost in thought, the worries fade,
In twilight's hush, our hearts cascade.

The horizon glows with muted hues,
A promise kept, as night ensues.
Holding moments that linger near,
In twilight's embrace, we find our cheer.

With every breath, a new story starts,
Beneath the veil, where magic imparts.
In the stillness, our spirits unite,
Embracing the dance of day and night.

Moments Suspended in Dust

In the golden light we sift,
Fragments of time drift slow,
Whispers of laughter softly lift,
Echoes of where we used to go.

Particles dance in the air,
Memories held in a single swirl,
Each grain a story laid bare,
The past and present in a twirl.

Through the haze, we search and find,
Treasures hidden in the gloom,
Remnants of a once bright mind,
Dust motes flicker, life resumes.

Captured moments, like a breath,
Suspended in the void of time,
Every silence hints of depth,
A fragile, transient rhyme.

And in this quiet, we will dwell,
Finding joy in the unseen,
In the stillness, stories swell,
Life reflected in a dream.

The Language of a Thousand Footfalls

Every step tells a tale,
Of journeys made, paths worn thin,
From whispered hopes to a wail,
Traces left where we have been.

The forest listens, branches sway,
Rustling secrets of the night,
Each footfall speaks in its own way,
A chorus woven soft yet bright.

Across the sands, a soft refrain,
Soft prints echoing the past,
Memories linger, joy and pain,
In every shadow that we cast.

Through cities crowded, noise and haste,
In alleys dark or streets so wide,
The rhythm of life, a sacred taste,
A symphony where dreams abide.

And when the dawn breaks clear and bright,
Each footfall leads to new desires,
A testament to endless flight,
The beating heart of life inspires.

When Shadows Dance on Parched Earth

Under the sun's relentless gaze,
The ground, a canvas cracked and bare,
Yet shadows twist in games they play,
    A fleeting grace, an art so rare.

Silent witnesses of the day,
They stretch and ripple with the breeze,
In-between the light's harsh way,
    A dance of solace, sweet reprieves.

With every dusk, they come alive,
A gentle tease of dusk's embrace,
In twilight's glow, they weave and thrive,
    Their fleeting forms a sacred space.

And though the earth may long for rain,
In every shadow, life abounds,
Beauty found in stark terrain,
    A quiet strength in solemn grounds.

So let the shadows guide the night,
Where hope can linger, softly churn,
In darkness, even faintest light,
Will dance, and from the silence, learn.

Beneath the Surface of Silence

In the hush where whispers play,
Layers fold like sheets of lace,
Hearts unspoken find their way,
Beneath the quiet, hidden grace.

The stillness holds a sacred space,
Emotions steep in silent pools,
Memories float, they interlace,
In silence deep, the spirit cools.

Each breath a movement, soft and slight,
A tapestry of dreams unspun,
In shadows deep, we find the light,
Where quietude embraces fun.

Through tranquil moments, time stands still,
Echoing softly, murmured sighs,
A fragile thread of unspent will,
In the silence, our truth lies.

And so we dive, we learn to hear,
Beneath the surface, voices rise,
In every pause, we draw so near,
The beauty found in quiet ties.

Hushed Footsteps on Ancient Paths

Through the woods, they softly tread,
Echoes linger, stories bred.
Whispers of the earth unfold,
Secrets in the silence told.

Leaves beneath their weary feet,
Time stands still in this retreat.
Guided by the faintest light,
Journeys woven through the night.

Footsteps tracing distant dreams,
Where the past and present gleam.
Ancient roots and starlit skies,
In the hush, the spirit flies.

Night enfolds the wandering soul,
In this place, they find their role.
With each step, a tale begins,
On ancient paths where time spins.

In stillness, magic weaves its thread,
In every whisper, joy and dread.
Hushed footsteps speak to the wise,
In the heart where memory lies.

Murmurs of the Wind's Caress

Gentle breezes softly sigh,
Carrying dreams that drift and fly.
Whispers of a world unseen,
Dance with shadows, bright and green.

Through the trees, the secrets weave,
Nature's pulse, a life to cleave.
Every gust, a soft embrace,
Bringing warmth to every place.

Murmurs flow like streams of gold,
Telling tales both new and old.
In the silence of the night,
Wind's caress, a pure delight.

Floating notes of sweet refrain,
Echoes linger, joy and pain.
Krasks of solitude entwined,
By the whispering breeze aligned.

In the hush, the spirit finds,
Songs that heal, that bind all minds.
Murmurs of a timeless grace,
In the wind's soft, warm embrace.

Shadows Cast by the Fading Sun

Longing glances stretch and fade,
As twilight claims the day's parade.
Shadows lengthen, soft and grand,
Holding secrets in the sand.

Silhouettes against the glow,
A dance of light, a quiet show.
Fleeting moments whisper low,
As dusk begins its gentle flow.

Fading hues of gold and red,
Paint the sky where dreams are bred.
In the twilight's tender sweep,
Shadows beckon, secrets keep.

Silent stories, dusk unveiled,
Through the night, the heart is hailed.
Beneath the stars, we weave our fate,
In shadows cast, we meditate.

Time slips softly into night,
While shadows dance in fading light.
Echoes from the day's retreat,
In their arms, we find our seat.

The Quiet Realm of Shifting Tides

Whispers rise from the ocean deep,
In quiet realms where secrets sleep.
Shifting sands, a lullaby,
Waves embrace the endless sky.

Salt and seafoam swirl and play,
As tides of time drift far away.
In this realm, the heart will soar,
Where every wave reveals much more.

Murmurs of the sea, so wise,
Carrying dreams beneath the skies.
Tidal pulls and gentle sways,
Guide the spirits through the days.

In the twilight, shadows glide,
Among the waves, we bide our stride.
Nature sings her softest song,
In this realm, we all belong.

Lost in thought, the world fades,
As the ocean's symphony cascades.
In the quiet of shifting tides,
Our hearts find solace, love abides.

The Poetry of Still Moments

In the hush of twilight's glow,
Time stands still, a gentle show.
Whispers dance upon the breeze,
Captured souls, like falling leaves.

Each heartbeat marks a soothing pause,
Nature's song without a cause.
Eyes closed tight, we breathe it in,
In this silence, we transcend.

A flicker caught within the light,
Dreams take flight on velvet night.
Moments linger, sweet and pure,
In stillness, we find allure.

Beneath the stars, our spirits soar,
Life unfolds, we want for more.
Here beneath the cosmic beam,
We rest within our waking dream.

Muffled Cries of a Dying Flame

In shadows deep where embers wane,
Flickers lost in a soft refrain.
Muffled cries of warmth once bold,
Now fade beneath the night so cold.

A hearth once bright, now flickering low,
Echoes linger as memories flow.
Smoke curls gently into the air,
A silent goodbye, a whispered prayer.

Through the darkness, shadows creep,
Promises made in dreams we keep.
Yet, in the silence, hope remains,
A spark still glows, despite the pains.

Each sigh a story left untold,
Each flicker speaks of warmth so bold.
In the quiet, love can still find,
A way to mend a heart, entwined.

When Footfalls Fade into Glistening Grain

The wheat fields sway in the golden sun,
Footfalls fade when the day is done.
A trail of whispers in the hushed land,
Leaving behind just a gentle hand.

Each grain a memory, soft and sweet,
Where laughter danced and heartbeat meets.
The sky spills colors, a painter's delight,
As day transforms softly into night.

Beneath the vast, eternal sky,
We walk in silence, you and I.
Nature's canvas, painted serene,
In glistening grain, we find our sheen.

As dusk descends with a twilight hymn,
We trace our steps on a pathway dim.
In every shadow, a story resides,
In stillness, our gentle pride.

Subtle Movements in the Vast Expanse

Among the stars, a dance unfolds,
In gentle whispers, the universe holds.
Subtle movements, a cosmic chant,
Awakens dreams where stardust plant.

The night sky breathes with tranquil grace,
Time drifts softly in this sacred space.
Each flicker tells of journeys wide,
In this expanse, we bide our stride.

Galaxies twist in a silent blur,
A symphony plays, as galaxies stir.
In every heartbeat, vastness thrives,
In subtle movements, the soul derives.

The universe hums a melodic sound,
In stillness, our wandering spirits are found.
With open hearts, we share our plight,
In the vast expanse, we find our light.

Breaths of Eternity in Wide Expanse

In the vastness, whispers call,
Gentle winds that sway and fall.
Time's embrace in every breath,
Echoing life, defying death.

Stars align in silent night,
Guiding souls to find their light.
With every pulse, the world awakes,
In stillness, the heart aches.

Moments dance in endless flow,
Like rivers deep where dreamers go.
Each heartbeat sings a timeless song,
In this expanse, we all belong.

Endless horizons, whispers of fate,
With every step, we navigate.
In the twilight, shadows blend,
Breaths of eternity without end.

The Secrets Carried by Ancient Winds

Through the valleys, stories roam,
Carried softly, far from home.
Whispers of ages long gone by,
Secrets held beneath the sky.

The winds compose a symphony,
Of lost dreams and history.
Rustling leaves and songs of trees,
Share their tales with every breeze.

In the twilight, shadows play,
Tracing paths of yesterday.
Fingertips brush against the past,
A dance of memories held steadfast.

Beneath the weight of endless skies,
Voices echo, never die.
Each gust brings forth a soft sigh,
In the secrets where they lie.

Shadows of Serenity on Bitter Soil

In gardens grown from bitter sound,
Serenity's grace can still be found.
Shadows linger, tales unfold,
Of hearts that brave both fire and cold.

Amidst the thorns, blooms take flight,
Finding beauty in darkest night.
With every whisper, hope persists,
In fragile hearts, love still exists.

Bitter soil, yet dreams take root,
Through the struggle, life looks cute.
Shadows bear the weight of time,
Yet in darkness, there's a rhyme.

Softly dusk turns to dawn,
New beginnings lightly drawn.
From every shadow, strength will rise,
Serenity blooms beneath the skies.

Chasing Echoes of a Still Heart

In quiet corners, echoes play,
Whispers of a brighter day.
A still heart beats with steady grace,
Chasing love in time and space.

Every sigh, a note of hope,
Binding souls with threads to cope.
In the silence, dreams resound,
Where true courage can be found.

Like shadows dancing 'neath the moon,
Chasing echoes, we find our tune.
With each heartbeat, stories weave,
In the stillness, we believe.

Light and shadow, intertwined,
In this silence, hearts aligned.
Chasing echoes, we discover,
In stillness, we find each other.

Secrets of the Wind-Carved Lines

Whispers drift through ancient pines,
Stories etched in weathered stones.
Carried by the breeze that twines,
Silent secrets, lost yet known.

Fingers trace the paths once trod,
Nature's canvas, endless lore.
In every curve, a silent nod,
To timeless truths that we explore.

Moonlight dances on the ground,
Illuminating tales of old.
In the stillness, wisdom found,
A universe of dreams retold.

Let the echoes guide your heart,
In the whispers of the night.
Every gust, a work of art,
Painting shadows, breathing light.

Through the trees, the stories flow,
Of love, of loss, and endless strife.
Listen close, and soon you'll know,
In each line, the breath of life.

Fading Echoes of Yesterday's Gaze

Memories linger, soft and sweet,
In the dusk, they wane and sigh.
Shadows stretch with weary feet,
Hints of laughter passing by.

Faded photographs in hand,
Time recedes like whispered dreams.
Moments drift like grains of sand,
Slipping through our silent seams.

Voices hush as twilight nears,
Every glance a fleeting spark.
In the fading light, our fears,
Meet the beauty of the dark.

In the silence, echoes sigh,
Carrying the weight of time.
With every breath, we learn to fly,
Through the verses, soft and prime.

Holding tight to what we've lost,
Each memory a precious gem.
In the shadows, love will cost,
Yet forever we ascend.

The Soft Embrace of Twilight

As the sun dips below the line,
A tender hush envelops all.
In twilight's arms, the stars align,
With every light, shadows fall.

Gentle whispers fill the air,
Colors bleed into the night.
In this moment, free from care,
Hearts awaken to soft light.

Crickets chirp a lullaby,
Nature's pulse in rhythmic flow.
The day gives way, and time will fly,
Into dusk's warm, sweet tableau.

In the blending of the hues,
Dreams arise like fireflies bright.
In each heart, the promise brews,
Of new beginnings in the night.

So breathe deep the fading glow,
Let the night your spirit lace.
In twilight's calm, our lives bestow,
A gentle touch, a soft embrace.

Cloaked in Shadows of Stillness

Quiet whispers cloak the night,
In shadows, secrets softly tread.
Stillness wraps the world in light,
As dreams linger, half unsaid.

The moon drapes silver on the ground,
Silhouettes dance in soft refrain.
Within the hush, a heart is found,
In every breath, a sweet disdain.

Leaves rustle with the ghostly grace,
Echoing tales of distant lands.
Time weaves threads through empty space,
Binding moments with gentle hands.

In this realm where silence reigns,
Every heartbeat is a song.
Through the dark, the spirit gains,
An understanding, deep and strong.

Hold this peace within your soul,
Embrace the shadows as your guide.
For in stillness, we become whole,
Cloaked in dreams where we can hide.

The Ghosts of Lost Footsteps

Whispers wander through the lane,
Faint echoes of love and pain.
Sunsets fade on a weary ground,
In silence, lost hopes are found.

Shadows dance where dreams once played,
Memories linger, softly swayed.
Footprints vanish in twilight's glow,
Leaving stories we barely know.

They beckon gently as night draws near,
Tales of laughter, hints of fear.
Each step marked by a fleeting glance,
In the dark, the past will dance.

With every sigh, the echoes strive,
To remind us that we're alive.
Ghosts of the past, both bright and dim,
Whispering secrets on a whim.

Beneath the stars, their stories weave,
In every heart, they take their leave.
For in the shadows, hope can gleam,
The ghosts of lost footsteps, a dream.

Dawn's Palette on a Washed Canvas

Soft brush strokes of golden light,
Chase away the remnants of night.
A canvas wakes in hues so bright,
Dawn's embrace, a wondrous sight.

Crimson whispers in the breeze,
Awakening the silent trees.
Lavender skies and blush of rose,
Nature's art in splendid prose.

Each color tells a brand new tale,
Of sunlit paths where dreams prevail.
The world adorned in gentle grace,
Time's tender touch, an intimate space.

As shadows fade to distant gray,
The heart begins a brand new day.
In dawn's palette, hope declares,
Life begins anew, unawares.

So linger long in morning's glow,
Embrace the light, let your spirit flow.
For in each dawn, a chance to see,
The beauty in life's artistry.

Solitude Amongst Endless Undulations

Waves of the heart, they rise and fall,
In solitude's grasp, we hear the call.
Endless hills, a lonesome plea,
Whispers of wind, setting us free.

Mountains loom like dreams untold,
Veiled in stories, both new and old.
In quiet moments, truths emerge,
As gentle tides begin to surge.

The horizon stretches far and wide,
A canvas for thoughts we cannot hide.
Each ripple echoes in our core,
Seeking solace, wanting more.

In nature's arms, we find our place,
Beneath the clouds, in time and space.
Amongst the undulations we roam,
Finding peace in the journey home.

So let the solitude gently weave,
A tapestry of dreams we believe.
In every rise and every dip,
Life's precious moments we shall grip.

Murmurs of Memory in the Grit

In the dust where shadows dwell,
Murmurs rise, they weave a spell.
Fragments of time, they softly cling,
To the grit, where memories sing.

Voices echo through the haze,
Painting pictures of bygone days.
With every breath, the past appears,
Flowing forth in whispered tears.

In the alleys, the heart takes flight,
Chasing dreams into the night.
Echoes shimmer like stars in black,
Guiding footsteps to the track.

Grit and grace unite as one,
Stories linger, never done.
Through the chaos, we sift and find,
The beauty buried in the blind.

So let the murmurs softly guide,
The memories that we cannot hide.
For in the grit, life's canvas holds,
A tapestry of stories bold.

Boundless Horizons of the Unspoken

In whispers carried by the breeze,
Dreams take flight beyond the trees.
Unseen paths stretch wide and far,
Guiding souls like a distant star.

Words unvoiced and tales untold,
Echo softly, brave and bold.
In every heart a story swells,
Of secret worlds, of magic spells.

Mountains loom and rivers flow,
Where thoughts are free, and wild winds blow.
Unraveled thoughts, like clouds above,
Shape the silence, weave the love.

Horizons dance with vibrant hues,
A canvas filled with endless views.
In the void, we find our song,
A melody that's lived too long.

Boundless dreams await our gaze,
In every heart, a silent blaze.
Together we will find our way,
Through unspoken words that sway.

Reflections in the Grainy Void

In shadows thick, where echoes dwell,
Reflections cast a timeless spell.
Faces fade in whispered light,
Grainy void, both deep and bright.

Moments captured, lost in time,
Fragments held in silent rhyme.
The past lingers like soft mist,
In every glimpse, a fleeting twist.

Waves of memory crash and swell,
In the void, stories weave and tell.
Each ripple bears a silent cry,
A love once felt, now drifting by.

Colors blend, and shadows play,
A dance of night that greets the day.
In the grainy depths we seek
The truth that hides, though hearts are weak.

In every spark, a life unfolds,
A thousand tales in whispers told.
In the void, we find the light,
Reflections guide us through the night.

Footfalls of Forgotten Journeys

On winding paths where stories roam,
Footfalls trace a path back home.
Echoing through the dust of time,
Each step a whisper, each path a rhyme.

Forgotten tales in bramble hide,
Voices lost, but hearts abide.
Footprints scattered like fallen leaves,
In the silence, memory weaves.

Through fields of gold and valleys wide,
Journeys echo, side by side.
In every glance the past resounds,
In every heart, a journey found.

The road ahead, with skies so blue,
Holds the dreams of me and you.
Through every trial, every cheer,
Footfalls guide us, drawing near.

With every step, the story grows,
Unknown paths where adventure flows.
Together we will brave the night,
With footfalls echoing in the light.

The Tapestry of Sunlit Silence

In quiet dawns where shadows creep,
Sunlit silence cradles deep.
Threads of light in golden beams,
Weaving harmonies of dreams.

Amidst the still, where whispers lie,
Nature breathes a gentle sigh.
Each leaf a note, each breeze a song,
In the silence, we belong.

Colors blend in warm embrace,
Time slows down to grace each space.
In the tapestry, we find our way,
Through sunlit paths at break of day.

Moments linger, soft and bright,
Painting shadows with the light.
In every thread, a story spun,
In every heartbeat, life's begun.

Together we will weave and bind,
The tapestry of heart and mind.
In sunlit silence, hand in hand,
We find our peace in a radiant land.

The Poetry of an Empty Horizon

In twilight's grasp, the colors blend,
Soft whispers of the day descend.
A canvas wide, with not a trace,
Of footprints left to mark this space.

The sun dips low, in gold and grey,
Where dreams and shadows often play.
Silent sighs from ocean waves,
Embrace the hush of evening's saves.

Clouds drift lightly, secrets hold,
Their stories weaved in threads of gold.
A vast expanse, where hopes take wing,
The horizon beckons, softly sings.

Stars arrive, a distant glow,
In the quiet night, they gently flow.
Each twinkle speaks, a silent verse,
Of endless dreams, the universe.

In this vast realm, I stand alone,
Yet in my heart, the wild has grown.
The poetry of night, so clear,
In the empty space, I disappear.

Each Grain Holds a Story

Upon the shore, the grains align,
Each one a tale of salt, and brine.
Time's soft hand has shaped their form,
In whispers light, they shift and swarm.

The sun-kissed sands of summers past,
In every grain, a shadow cast.
Fragments of journeys, lost and found,
In the dance of tides, their voices sound.

Footsteps fade but stories stay,
In every shift, they find their way.
From ancient shores to distant lands,
Each grain whispers of time's demands.

Beneath the skies, where dreams collide,
And heartbeats echo with the tide.
These tiny stones, though small in size,
Hold vast horizons, under skies.

In every grain, a world to see,
Of laughter shared, and wild glee.
In the silence of the shore's embrace,
Each grain holds stories time won't erase.

Whispers of the Dunes

In the quiet of the desert's breath,
Where golden dunes hide tales of death.
Soft winds carry forgotten fears,
In whispered tones, they sing of years.

The sun may blaze, the shadows play,
But secrets here won't fade away.
With every shift, the sands conspire,
To hold the lost, the dreams, the fire.

Beneath the surface, stories kept,
Of wanderers who once have wept.
The dunes rise high, like ancient tomes,
With every grain, a link to homes.

Night descends, a silver veil,
In fragrant air, the stars unveil.
The echoes of the dunes arise,
In quiet night, beneath the skies.

A tapestry of time unfolds,
In every grain, a journey holds.
Whispers of the dunes, so true,
In sands of time, our dreams renew.

Secrets Beneath the Grain

Beneath the surface, life concealed,
In every grain, a fate revealed.
Whispers linger, soft and low,
As tides of time begin to flow.

In the quiet, shadows blend,
Stories hide, waiting to mend.
Each grain a part of earth's embrace,
Holds a secret, knows its place.

Time flows like water, ever near,
What was lost finds home, my dear.
In every fold, a tale spun tight,
Of sunlit days and endless night.

Unseen, the magic softly hums,
In every step, the past becomes.
A legacy of sand and stone,
In nature's arms, we're not alone.

Secrets waiting, patiently dressed,
In layers deep, the heart's request.
Beneath the grain, we find our way,
In whispers soft, both night and day.

Gentle Tides of Yesterday's Echo

Whispers of waves caress the shore,
Memories linger, wanting more.
Sandcastles built, now washed away,
In the tide's dance, they gently sway.

Footprints fade in twilight's gleam,
Echoes of laughter, a distant dream.
The sun dips low, the sky aglow,
In the sea's embrace, time moves slow.

Seabirds call as the day does close,
In salty air, a peaceful prose.
Each drop tells tales of love and loss,
The ocean's heart, a silent gloss.

Ripples carry whispers of the past,
Moments unbroken, memories cast.
Gentle tides sing sweet refrains,
In the ebb and flow, we find our chains.

Stars awaken in velvet skies,
Mirrors of dreams in countless eyes.
The night embraces, the world feels wide,
As we float on waves, in time we glide.

The Sound of Dreams Drifting

Gentle sighs of sleep's embrace,
Dreams take flight, a sacred space.
Whispers weave through night's soft veil,
Echoes of wishes, a soothing tale.

Stars like lanterns blink with grace,
Guiding hopes in a timeless race.
Each heartbeat beats in rhythmic flow,
To melodies only dreamers know.

Clouds cradle thoughts, both wild and free,
Carrying stories across the sea.
Soft-like feathers, unbound and light,
Drifting gently into the night.

Sleep's embrace, a tranquil hold,
As secrets of heart and mind unfold.
In the silence, spirits play,
In the sound of dreams, we drift away.

Morning whispers, the dawn appears,
Waking visions, dispelling fears.
In the light, we find our way,
The sound of dreams will gently stay.

Calm Respite in Nature's Embrace

Beneath the trees, where shadows fall,
Nature whispers, a soothing call.
Birds in flight weave through the air,
In every breath, peace lingers there.

Leaves dance lightly, a gentle breeze,
Carrying scents of blooming trees.
In the stillness, hearts attune,
To nature's pulse beneath the moon.

Streams babble sweetly, echoing life,
In harmony, with joy rife.
Rays of sunlight break through the green,
In this calm, our spirits glean.

Mountains stand, timeless and strong,
Guardians of earth, where we belong.
In every crack, in every stone,
A testament of nature's throne.

Gathered moments in nature's fold,
Stories of courage, softly told.
In nature's embrace, we find a place,
Where solace blooms, and dreams interlace.

The Philosophy of Still Waters

Reflective pools hold thoughts so deep,
In stillness, secrets quietly seep.
Time pauses here, the world feels near,
In silence, wisdom starts to clear.

Rippling waters, a mirrored view,
Capturing moments, both old and new.
Each ripple tells of a journey far,
A universe held beneath a star.

In tranquil depths, the heart does speak,
To find the strength in being weak.
Flowing thoughts like currents glide,
Carving paths where feelings hide.

The stillness offers a gentle pause,
A chance to reflect, to see the cause.
With every gaze into the pond,
The mind expands, our fears respond.

In the quiet, find your truth,
Carefully sip from the well of youth.
In still waters, the soul takes flight,
Navigating through the silent night.

Veils of Quietude in the Barren

Beneath the sun's relentless glare,
The sands stretch far and wide,
Whispers of stillness fill the air,
In this vast and empty tide.

Shadows dance on dunes so tall,
A fleeting touch, a ghostly trace,
In the silence, we hear the call,
Of time's gentle, slow embrace.

Footprints linger, fading fast,
Memories etched in golden grain,
The present joins the echoes past,
In this solemn, sandy domain.

A sky that fades from blue to gray,
And clouds that drift like dreams untold,
In the stillness, night takes sway,
As stars replace the sun's bold gold.

So here I stand, a witness true,
To the beauty wrapped in quiet veils,
In the barren, life starts anew,
In the whispers of ancient trails.

Tides of Time on Arid Shores

The waves of time, they kiss the land,
In rhythms soft yet deftly strong,
Each grain of sand, a tale unplanned,
A melody where memories belong.

The sun retreats, the shadows grow,
As twilight weaves its dusky thread,
With every tide, the past will flow,
Where dreams and echoes gently tread.

The shorelines shift, the winds do speak,
In whispers rich with secrets old,
On arid sands, the hearts may seek,
The stories hidden, still untold.

Moonlight dances on the crest,
Illuminating paths unseen,
In the quiet, we find our quest,
On shores where time and hope convene.

So let the sea embrace our souls,
With every breath, let us align,
For in the tides, the heart consoles,
A timeless dance, divine, benign.

Sighs of the Wind Through Shifting Landscapes

The wind carries whispers, soft and rare,
Through valleys wide and hills that rise,
Each sigh an echo, light as air,
Across the land, beneath the skies.

It weaves through mountains, a gentle stream,
Brushing the leaves with tender grace,
In shifting hues, we find the dream,
A dance of shadows on nature's face.

Through fragrant fields where wildflowers sway,
The breeze enchants with tales of old,
In every rustle, secrets play,
As time unfurls its threads of gold.

The canyons hum with ancient lore,
As currents guide the wandering song,
In the sighs of the wind, we explore,
The bond of the earth, forever strong.

So let us listen, hearts open wide,
To the whispers of the world, so grand,
For in each sigh, we shall abide,
In harmony with the shifting land.

The Invisible Symphony of the Dunes

In the stillness, music flows,
A symphony of sand and light,
Where every grain in silence knows,
The rhythm born from day to night.

The dunes arise like waves of grace,
With curves that cradle fleeting dreams,
In their embrace, we find our place,
In the softest, whispered themes.

As twilight falls, the shadows play,
A theater where the night takes flight,
The dunes compose an ode to stay,
In secrets shared between the night.

Each footstep echoes, soft and low,
In time's embrace, we drift along,
The heartbeats match the lunar glow,
In harmony, we craft our song.

So close your eyes, and hear the sound,
Of silence turned to vibrant hue,
For in the dunes, the lost are found,
In the invisible we pursue.

Unvoiced Sentiments Amidst the Dust

In corners dim where shadows play,
Whispers linger, lost in grey.
Hearts entwined in silence speak,
Dreams now faded, so to seek.

Words unsaid, a heavy hue,
Chasing moments, few but true.
Memories fade like grains of sand,
In this quiet, where we stand.

Beneath the weight of time's embrace,
Silent echoes fill the space.
Yet in the dust, a spark remains,
Of unvoiced love, and silent pains.

Through the years, we try to find,
Fragments of a heart entwined.
In the stillness, we confide,
Unvoiced truths we try to hide.

In this realm of lost desires,
Burn soft embers, fading fires.
Through the silence, we perceive,
Unvoiced sentiments we believe.

Time's Gentle Caress on the Forgotten

Whispers of the past unfold,
Stories of the brave and bold.
Time caresses every face,
Leaves behind its soft embrace.

Memories drift like autumn leaves,
Carried softly on the breeze.
In quiet corners, shadows stir,
Echoes of what once was hers.

Time, a thief with gentle hands,
Wears away the dreams and plans.
Yet in the crevices of night,
Hope glimmers, faint but bright.

Every wrinkle tells a tale,
Of laughter, love, and dreams that pale.
In stillness, we recall the glow,
Of brighter days that long ago.

As we walk this winding road,
Time's embrace, both light and load.
In forgotten moments, we find,
The gentle touch that warms the mind.

Reflections in the Sands of the Past

Footprints drawn on golden shore,
Fleeting echoes, here no more.
In the sands, the stories lie,
Felting whispers from the sky.

Each grain holds a memory dear,
Of laughter shared and of each tear.
Reflections dance in sunlit glow,
Tracing paths we used to know.

Time erodes yet never fades,
Moments cherished, love cascades.
In the silence, we are found,
As tides bring forth that sacred ground.

Lost in thought, we wander still,
Through the corridors of will.
In the waves, the stories blend,
Reflections that will never end.

With each tide, a chance to see,
Lives we've lived so carelessly.
In the sands, we trace the past,
In the hearts, the memories last.

A Lullaby Under the Stars

Beneath the quilt of midnight skies,
Softly hum the crickets' lullabies.
Moonlight dances on the lake,
Whispers of dreams that softly wake.

Glistening stars twinkle bright,
Holding secrets in the night.
Each breath of wind a gentle sigh,
Carried forth as time drifts by.

Nestled close, the world feels right,
Cradled in this velvet night.
In the hush, our hearts align,
Telling tales, both yours and mine.

As shadows wane, we drift away,
In the magic that holds sway.
With hope, we chase a day anew,
Underneath this sky so blue.

Close your eyes and dream a dream,
Under stars that softly gleam.
In this moment, pure and rare,
A lullaby hangs in the air.

The Unraveled Threads of Dune Tales

Amidst the shifting sands they lie,
Stories woven, lost in time.
Echoes of whispers, soft and shy,
Dune tales drift in a rhythmic rhyme.

Fingers trace the ancient paths,
Each grain a memory, rich and deep.
Carried by winds, the laughter lasts,
Secrets of travelers, awake from sleep.

Nightfall paints the desert sky,
Stars align with stories spun.
Migrations dance, as dreams go by,
In every shimmer, there's a run.

Cloaked in shadows, tales unfold,
Figures dance in the moonlight.
The dunes hold tales of bold,
In silence beneath the starlight.

So listen close to the winds' soft sigh,
Embrace the whispers, let them guide.
Through every dune and every high,
In the tales, our souls abide.

A Silence Wrapped in Sunlight

In golden hues, the world stands still,
A hush blankets the vibrant field.
Sunlight kisses, warm as will,
In the quiet, all secrets are revealed.

Birdsong dances on tender air,
Moments blend in soft embrace.
Time drips slowly, without a care,
In the silence, we find our place.

Shadows stretch upon the ground,
Fingers of light weave through the trees.
In this reverie, peace is found,
Whispers of joy ride on the breeze.

The heart beats in a gentle sway,
Nature's rhythm, a soothing balm.
In this stillness, worries stray,
Wrapped in sunlight, the world feels calm.

So breathe in deep, let moments flow,
In this silence, find your song.
Let sunlight guide where thoughts may go,
Wrapped in warmth, where we belong.

Submerged Thoughts in Gritty Embrace

Dive into the shadows cast,
Where gritty dreams take shape and form.
Thoughts submerged, echoes of the past,
In the depths, we weather the storm.

A canvas stained with hidden fears,
Crimson tides of emotions swell.
In murky waters, shed the tears,
Find the stories we dare not tell.

Reach for the pearls that dwell below,
Each glimmer a spark of the heart.
Through tumult and toil, we grow,
In the muck, we create our art.

The embrace of grit, a lover's hold,
Forging strength from fragile thread.
In every struggle, we find gold,
Shaped by currents we bravely tread.

So sink beneath, make peace with the grime,
For in the depths, our spirits rise.
Submerged thoughts become sublime,
In gritty embrace, we touch the skies.

Whispers of the Unseen Traveler

In the shadows, footsteps fade,
An unseen traveler roams the night.
Carrying echoes, memories made,
Whispers transform, taking flight.

Cities pause for the tales they bring,
Stories woven in the fabric of time.
As twilight's curtain starts to cling,
Each moment pulses with silent chime.

Through alleyways, under stars aglow,
The path winds where few have trod.
The heart beats loud, yet soft, like snow,
Invisible threads connect with a nod.

With every corner, new dreams await,
Life vibrant, in stillness it pulses.
An unseen traveler shapes fate,
In subtle wonder, the world repulses.

So listen close for the whispers near,
In the quiet, all stories reveal.
The unseen traveler holds us dear,
Through every breath, our lives congeal.

When Time Stopped in the Wilderness

The trees held whispers, soft and light,
As shadows danced in fading light.
A rustle echoed through the air,
Where nature paused, and none would dare.

The crickets paused, the summer's hum,
In stillness deep, no steady drum.
The stream ran slow, a hidden grace,
While moments slipped to darker space.

Stars blinked down, a distant cheer,
As midnight wrapped the world so dear.
With every breath, the wild drew near,
And time stood still, its path unclear.

The moonlight pooled upon the ground,
In silver shades, a world unbound.
The forest sighed, a gentle tune,
In twilight's glow and quiet's swoon.

In this realm where moments freeze,
Life dances soft upon the breeze.
A timeless echo, pure, profound,
In wilderness, forever found.

Glistening Traces of Moonlit Paths

Upon the path where shadows tease,
Moonbeams shimmer through the trees.
Each step a dream, each breath a sigh,
Where starlit whispers fill the sky.

Silver glistens on leaves so bright,
Guiding wanderers through the night.
A tapestry of light unfolds,
As ancient stories softly told.

In tangled roots beneath the stars,
The earth embraces, healing scars.
Each trail reveals a sacred dance,
In moonlit nights, we find our chance.

The world feels hushed, the air serene,
As shadows fade, and paths are seen.
With every heartbeat, dreams align,
In silver glow, our spirits shine.

Glistening traces mark the way,
Through nightly whispers, night and day.
In nature's arms, forever free,
The moonlight calls, calling to me.

The Calm After the Storm

With thunder spent and skies turned clear,
The world exhales, the end draws near.
Raindrops linger on blades of grass,
A shattered calm as moments pass.

The sun peeks through, a golden ray,
Cleansing shadows from yesterday.
In fragrant air, the freshness sings,
A symphony of gentle things.

Clouds drift away like fleeting dreams,
Painting the sky with vibrant beams.
And nature stirs, reborn in grace,
As life returns to every place.

Birds take flight in joyful arcs,
With melodies that fill the parks.
In tranquil moments, peace is drawn,
The calm emerges with the dawn.

A heartbeat strong, a breath anew,
In stillness found, beneath the blue.
The storm has passed, the world shall thrive,
In quiet bliss, we come alive.

Still Waters in a Desert's Heart

A hidden pool beneath the sun,
Where dry winds whisper, life undone.
The surface rests like polished glass,
Reflecting skies where moments pass.

Around the edge, the silence sings,
As fragile dreams take flight on wings.
The desert blooms with colors rare,
In stillness held, beyond compare.

Beneath the stars, the waters gleam,
A tranquil space where shadows dream.
In every ripple, secrets lie,
A world unfolds where echoes sigh.

The heart of sand holds life so dear,
In hidden depths, the stillness near.
With every breath, the silence speaks,
Where peace resides, the spirit seeks.

In tender grace, the waters flow,
Through arid lands, where soft winds blow.
Still waters in the desert's heart,
A whispered truth, a work of art.

Murmuring Specifications of the Serene

In the hush of twilight's shade,
Whispers of the night invade.
Leaves converse with gentle breeze,
Nature's sighs bring hearts at ease.

Stars blink in a velvet sky,
Moonbeams dance as shadows fly.
Crickets play a soothing tune,
In the arms of night, we swoon.

Clouds drift slow, a tranquil dream,
Softly glowing like a stream.
Promises linger in the air,
Love is hidden everywhere.

Each heartbeat a serene sound,
In this moment, peace is found.
Hand in hand, we wander far,
Guided softly by a star.

Let the world's noise fade away,
In this quiet, we shall stay.
Murmurs of the heart align,
In the calm, your soul's with mine.

When Dreams Dance on Golden Grains

Fields of amber sway and gleam,
Whispers rise from every dream.
Sunlight bathes the earth in gold,
   Stories waiting to be told.

Barefoot on the warming sand,
Childlike laughter, hand in hand.
Fingers trace the silky seams,
Awakening our boldest dreams.

In the twilight's soft embrace,
Time becomes a fleeting space.
Windswept thoughts on gentle air,
  Carry hopes beyond compare.

Dancing grains beneath our feet,
  Every step a chance to meet.
   Life's a tapestry we weave,
  In the moment, we believe.

Moonlit nights and sunrise hues,
  Inspiration born from views.
When we dream, the world expands,
  Magic's found in golden grains.

The Quiet Story of Celestial Sand

Beneath the stars, a tale unfolds,
In grains of sand, the past holds.
Each whisper of a timeless wave,
Crafts the story of the brave.

Footprints pressed in moonlit glow,
Mark the paths where dreamers go.
Silhouettes of lovers fade,
In the quiet, memories played.

Ebb and flow, the ocean's grace,
Waves of time, a soft embrace.
Secrets linger in the breeze,
Floating gently through the trees.

Stars, like storytellers, shine,
Guiding souls through space and time.
In celestial dust, we find,
Connections rich and intertwined.

As night deepens and shadows blend,
In every grain, dreams transcend.
The whispers of the moonlit strand,
Tell the quiet story of sand.

Tides of Tranquility in a Restless World

Oceans roar while hearts remain,
In the rush, we seek the plain.
Waves that crash on rocky shore,
Hold the peace we long for more.

In the chaos, find the calm,
Nature serves a soothing balm.
Beneath the tempest, whispers hide,
Quiet moments, waves abide.

Tides that pull and tides that sway,
Guide our hearts to brighter day.
In the dance of ebb and flow,
Finding solace in the show.

Stars above in perfect sync,
In their light, we pause and think.
In this restless world we roam,
The tide of peace will lead us home.

So let the oceans crash and roar,
We'll find tranquility in the core.
In the depths, our spirits soar,
Tides of calm forevermore.

Whispered Secrets of the Void

In shadows deep, where silence breathes,
Stars flicker softly, weaving eves.
Voices echo in the dark,
Secrets linger, a distant spark.

Among the emptiness, time does dance,
Holding stories in a trance.
Galaxies spiral, secrets twirl,
In the void, mysteries unfurl.

Whispers beckon from the night,
Guiding souls towards the light.
Ancient tales of worlds that fade,
In the silence, memories laid.

Beyond the edge, where dreams collide,
Truths emerge, no need to hide.
Winds of change softly sweep,
In the void, our promises keep.

Endless echoes, a cosmic song,
In the darkness, we belong.
Each whisper tells of paths untold,
In the void, our hearts are bold.

The Quietude of Woven Memories

In the quiet mist of yesterday,
Threads of time begin to sway.
Faded laughter fills the air,
A tapestry of love laid bare.

Golden hues of autumn's grace,
Softly touch a cherished face.
Each moment stitched, a gentle seam,
In the fabric of a waking dream.

Whispers of a sunset glow,
Memories like rivers flow.
Every stitch a tale to tell,
In the quietude, we dwell.

Time drifts softly, a feathered breeze,
Carrying echoes through the trees.
Woven threads entwined in fate,
In the sanctuary we create.

Present meets the past in light,
A dance that feels just right.
In the quietude, we find our way,
Amidst the woven dreams we lay.

Sandstorms and Solace

In the heart of dunes, whispers roam,
Sandstorms swirl, nature's own poem.
Amidst the chaos, a stillness grows,
In the tempest, quiet flows.

Grains of time slip through our hands,
Each one carries ancient lands.
In every swirl, a tale unfolds,
Of journeys against the holding molds.

Fleeting shadows in the golden light,
Guide us home through day and night.
Solace found in the barren space,
Desert whispers, a warm embrace.

Sand shifts softly beneath our feet,
In the storm, we find retreat.
Through the grit, our spirits rise,
In the quiet, the heart complies.

In solitude, we unearth the truth,
Sandstorms teach us of our youth.
Through the storm, a calm we gain,
In the chaos, there's no pain.

Mirage of Unfolding Dreams

In the horizon, visions gleam,
A mirage paints an endless dream.
Whispers call from lands afar,
Guiding hearts to where they are.

Beneath the stars, hopes ignite,
Fleeting visions in the night.
Every glance, a story shared,
In the silence, hearts laid bare.

Time unfolds like petals bloom,
In the darkness, dispelling gloom.
Dreams once lost return anew,
Mirages dance in shades of blue.

Along the journey, laughter rings,
In every moment, true joy springs.
Each step forward, a gentle glide,
In the mirage, we take pride.

Through the haze, our paths align,
In the twilight, our stars shine.
With opened hearts, we embrace the night,
In the mirage, we find our light.

Embrace of the Starlit Soil

In night's soft cradle, we lay low,
Beneath the whispers of a silver glow.
The earth cradles dreams, tender and bright,
Each heartbeat echoing in the gentle night.

Crickets serenade under a velvet sky,
While shadows dance as twilight draws nigh.
The soil warms softly, embracing our sighs,
In this sacred moment where eternity lies.

Stars weave stories in a cosmic thread,
Illuminating paths where our hearts dare tread.
A canopy of hope above, wide and clear,
In the embrace of the starlit soil, we adhere.

Beneath the vastness, all worries grow small,
In the embrace of nature, we find our call.
With hands intertwined, we breathe in the whole,
Alive in the wonder of the starlit soil.

As dawn hues blossom, dreams gently retreat,
Yet the starlit embrace remains bittersweet.
For in every echo, a part of us stays,
In the embrace of the starlit soil, forever ablaze.

Subtle Shifts of the Mirage

In the desert's heart, where illusions play,
The sun paints stories in shimmering sway.
Each grain of sand, a tale untold,
In subtle shifts, the mirage unfolds.

Waves of heat dance, distorting the view,
While secrets linger beneath skies of blue.
Footprints vanish, like dreams in the air,
The mirage whispers, but few would dare.

Cacti stand guard with a watchful eye,
As shadows stretch and the daylight draws by.
In this timeless space, reality bends,
Embracing the magic that never quite ends.

Winds weave through canyons with a sultry tune,
Crafting a symphony beneath the bright moon.
In the blink of the eye, landscapes may shift,
In subtle surrender, the horizons drift.

As twilight approaches, the colors ignite,
The mirage fades softly, bidding goodnight.
But in the heart's canvas, it forever stays,
In subtle shifts of the mirage, it plays.

Hushed Footprints on Forgotten Trails

Where shadows linger, and stories are spun,
Hushed footprints wander, a journey begun.
Each step a whisper, each breath a sigh,
On forgotten trails where memories lie.

Leaves rustle softly, like secrets exchanged,
Through tangled thickets, our paths rearranged.
The breeze carries echoes of laughter and tears,
As we trace the remnants of long-lost years.

Moss carpets old stones, a tapestry worn,
In quietude, we feel the warmth of the morn.
Nature's embrace, a gentle caress,
In hushed footsteps, we find our confess.

The woodland sings softly, a lullaby clear,
As sunlight dapples and beckons us near.
Each moment a gem, a treasure unveiled,
On forgotten trails, our love has sailed.

As twilight descends, we linger in grace,
In hush of the night, we find our place.
For just like the trails, our hearts intertwine,
In hushed footprints, forever we shine.

The Stillness Between Each Grain

In the hourglass moments that slip through our hands,
Lies the essence of life in soft, silent strands.
The stillness whispers where time holds its breath,
In the fleeting embrace of life and of death.

Each grain tells a story, both subtle and strong,
Of seasons that pass, of roots that belong.
In the gaps of our days, where silence may dwell,
The stillness beckons, casting its spell.

We linger in twilight, where shadows take flight,
In the calm of the dusk, all is bathed in light.
Every heartbeat echoes, a rhythm refined,
In the stillness between each grain, we find.

Moments float softly, like feathers in breeze,
Drawing us closer, inviting us to seize.
Within the pauses, the quiet unfolds,
In stillness, the universe patiently holds.

As stars begin twinkling, a gentle refrain,
We cherish the stillness, embracing the plain.
For in every silence, a treasure remains,
In the stillness between each grain, love sustains.

Gentle Ripples of a Timeworn Hourglass

Time trickles softly down,
Each grain a whispered tale.
Moments dance like shadows,
Fleeting, they leave a trail.

Hands of time, they gracefully sway,
Marking the paths we tread.
Within the glass, history stays,
Carried in whispers spread.

Memories slip through our fingers,
Echoes of laughter and sighs.
In the stillness, love lingers,
As moments softly rise.

Each flicker, a choice to behold,
Lessons learn, and hearts grow.
In the silence, stories unfold,
In the hourglass, we flow.

So cherish each gentle ripple,
Embrace the hours that pass.
In the grand, eternal temple,
Life's beauty, like glass.

Solitude in a Sea of Sand

A vast desert stretches wide,
Waves of gold beneath the sun.
In solitude, I confide,
Lost, but adventures begun.

Each grain a silent secret,
Buried deep beneath the light.
Whispers travel on the breeze,
Carrying echoes of night.

In the quiet, thoughts linger,
Like shadows cast by the noon.
With each step, I feel lighter,
The heart's tune, a soft tune.

Stars at dusk adorn the sky,
Mapping dreams in silver streams.
In the stillness, I can fly,
Awakening gentle themes.

Solitude, a precious friend,
Guiding through this barren land.
In stillness, I ascend,
Finding strength to understand.

Dreams Caught in Warm Breezes

Dreams flutter like autumn leaves,
Carried by whispers of air.
They dance in the twilight eves,
Floating without a care.

In the warmth of fading light,
Visions drift on golden haze.
They shimmer in the soft night,
Guided by time's gentle ways.

With each breath, a wish is born,
Caught in currents soft and sweet.
They rise with the blush of dawn,
As the world finds its heartbeat.

Through the branches, they wander,
Echoes of hopes untold.
In the quiet, I ponder,
The warmth of dreams unfold.

Embrace the breeze that surrounds,
Let dreams lead where they may.
In the heart's gentle sounds,
Find freedom in the sway.

The Weight of Unspoken Words

In silence, promises linger,
Heavy as shadows at dusk.
Thoughts weigh on tender fingers,
Binding ties with quiet husk.

Each glance, a tale unwritten,
Words held back, a silent plea.
In the stillness, hearts are smitten,
Yearning for what could be.

Walls built high with unvoiced fears,
Cracked by longing's gentle ache.
Behind the smiles, hidden tears,
In each pause, the silence breaks.

What is said can never capture,
The depth of what is concealed.
In the heart, a quiet rapture,
A truth that time has healed.

Let us break these woven bounds,
Lift the weight of what's unseen.
In the space of tender sounds,
Find the freedom in between.

Serenity Beneath the Starlit Sky

Underneath the silver glow,
A gentle breeze begins to flow.
Stars twinkle in the velvet night,
Whispers of peace in soft twilight.

Crickets sing their soothing tune,
While shadows dance beneath the moon.
A tranquil heart, a mind at ease,
In nature's arms, we find our peace.

The world slows down, the moments freeze,
In sacred stillness, we feel the breeze.
Time drifts softly, like flowing streams,
In the quiet, we chase our dreams.

Each breath a sigh, each sigh a prayer,
To touch the stars, to lose our care.
Under this vast expanse we stand,
Serenity held in nature's hand.

Night wraps around like a loving shawl,
In this haven, we find our all.
With starlit whispers, our spirits soar,
In serenity's embrace, forevermore.

Crystal Whispers of the Abyss

In shadows deep where secrets dwell,
The ocean's heart begins to swell.
Crystal whispers graze the ear,
Tales of wonders, stories clear.

Bubbles rise in shimmering dance,
Inviting us to take a chance.
Vast horizons, azure seas,
Holding dreams like drifting leaves.

From depths below, a haunting call,
Echoes through the watery hall.
Tides embrace with gentle grace,
A soothing balm for every face.

Stars beneath the waves ignite,
In realms where day meets moonlit night.
Glimmers swirl in silent bliss,
In crystal whispers, we find our wish.

The abyss holds its ancient lore,
A treasure trove of tales and more.
With every pulse, the sea will show,
How life's wonders ebb and flow.

Narratives Drifting on the Breeze

Gentle winds weave through the trees,
Carrying tales upon their knees.
Stories born from whispered sighs,
Of far-off lands and painted skies.

Leaves rustle with a soft refrain,
Echoing laughter, joy, and pain.
Each gust a memory set free,
Flowing through all of history.

Clouds gather, shapeshift in flight,
Painting dreams in the fading light.
The breeze ignites the heart's own fire,
As narratives call us to aspire.

In every breath, a canvas bold,
Stories of the brave and the old.
Through each journey, we find our way,
As whispers guide us day by day.

With every note, the wind will sing,
Of love, of loss, each hidden thing.
In the dance of air, life's tales align,
Narratives drifting, pure and divine.

Echoing Silences of a Distant Land

In quiet realms where shadows fall,
The silent echoes softly call.
Mountains rise in still repose,
Guarding secrets no one knows.

A landscape draped in twilight's haze,
Time stands still in forgotten ways.
Footprints linger where spirits trod,
In the silence, we sense the nod.

Whispers of wind trace ancient paths,
As nature's peace sweetly laughs.
Mysterious lands beneath the stars,
Where silence sings of distant wars.

Echoes dwell in every stone,
Soft reminders of lives once known.
In the hush, connection grows,
To the past, the heart bestows.

Each moment lingers, a sacred dance,
In echoing silence, we find our chance.
A distant land, a gentle tide,
In quietude, our souls abide.

Layers of Time in Undisturbed Grains

Whispers of ages lie in the sand,
Stories unfurling at nature's hand.
Each grain a memory, soft and profound,
Time's gentle touch, forever unbound.

Echoes of footsteps, where journeys begun,
In twilight's embrace, with the setting sun.
Layers of history, drifting like dreams,
Turning to echoes, lost in soft gleams.

Beneath the surface, life waits to rise,
An odyssey hidden from wandering eyes.
In shadows of moments, serenity waits,
Nature's great canvas, where time permeates.

With each gentle breeze, the past calls to play,
In whispers of silence, the heart finds its way.
A tapestry woven with each breath of air,
Layers of time whisper, if only we dare.

Together we tread this timeless expanse,
In the dance of the grains, we find our chance.
To honor the stories of ages gone by,
In layers of time, we learn how to fly.

Beneath the Canopy of Unbroken Silence

In the stillness, where shadows reside,
Nature's breath holds secrets inside.
Leaves whisper softly in hushed, gentle tones,
Beneath the canopy, the world atones.

Sunlight weaves patterns in vibrant array,
Painting soft moments that softly decay.
Echoes of stillness in branches above,
A refuge of calm, a temple of love.

Where every heartbeat blends with the earth,
And silence enfolds the sound of rebirth.
In layers of green, tranquility reigns,
Breaths of the forest, like soft, flowing chains.

Pulsing with life in a sacred embrace,
Time stands still in this hallowed space.
With every rustle, a story takes flight,
Beneath the silence, we find our light.

Each step through the shadows a journey anew,
In mysteries woven where skies blush with blue.
Beneath the canopy, all fears turn to dust,
In unbroken silence, we learn to trust.

Where the Sun Meets Peaceful Shores

Waves gently whisper, caressing the land,
Where the sun dips low, hand in hand.
Golden horizons, kissed by soft light,
A tranquil embrace as day turns to night.

Seagulls call out in joyous delight,
Dancing on currents, a jubilant flight.
Footprints in sand, stories etched by time,
Where the sun meets shores, a rhythm, a rhyme.

Tides ebb and flow with a calming grace,
Each moment a treasure, a sacred space.
Shores woven with dreams, both ancient and new,
In the heart of the ocean, a deep shade of blue.

Wanderers gather in twilight's soft glow,
Sharing their tales where the warm breezes blow.
Where laughter and whispers meld into one,
In the embrace of the sea, two souls become one.

As stars blanket skies in a shimmering hue,
The moon graces waters, reflecting the true.
Where the sun meets shores, love's journey unfolds,
In waves of devotion, eternity holds.

In the Shadows of the Golden Dunes

Whispers of sand, soft beneath our feet,
In shadows of dunes, where earth and sky meet.
Golden waves ripple, shifting with grace,
Secrets of history hidden in place.

As sunlight cascades over glistening peaks,
The language of silence is all that it speaks.
Each grain a story, a journey of old,
In the shadows, the mystery quietly unfolds.

Footprints of wanderers lost in the past,
In dunes that remember, where shadows are cast.
Nature's own canvas with textures so fine,
A tapestry woven with threads of divine.

Time dances slowly, each moment a gift,
In the stillness, we feel our spirits lift.
Echoes of laughter, of joy intertwined,
In golden shadows, our hearts are aligned.

As twilight approaches with colors ablaze,
The shadows grow longer, in a gentle haze.
In the realms of the dunes, our souls find their home,
In the whispers of sands, we are never alone.

www.ingramcontent.com/pod-product-compliance
Ingram Content Group UK Ltd.
Pitfield, Milton Keynes, MK11 3LW, UK
UKHW031957131224
452403UK00010B/488